DARE YOU N

AMAZING
JOKES

12 FOR YEAR OLD KIDS

Hilarious Joke Book Bursting with Hundreds of Awesome LOL Thigh Slappers, Riddles, Knock-Knocks & More!

TESSE ADAMS

HERE AT LAST!
We have taken the Try Not to Laugh
Challenge to the Next Level!

LOL   *LOL*

Introducing
The Dare You Not to Laugh Challenge™
for Tweens!
If surviving the tween years isn't
challenging enough, here comes the
best teen cringe-worthy collection
of jokes that are tween-themed
and designed to squeak out a LOL
or two! Don't miss out on all
the fun and eye rolls!

We Dare You Not to Laugh
or at least Smile!

LOL   *LOL*

5

What is the best way to get your mom's attention?

Sit down and look comfortable.

Little Bro: "I can't go to school today."

Big Bro: "Why?"

Little Bro: "I have hypothermia."

Little Bro: "I am too COOL to go to school."

What do history teachers talk about when they hang out?

The OLD DAYS!

How does a vampire start a letter?

TOMB it may concern...

Why should you never text the undead?

They always end up GHOSTING you.

Why should you be suspicious of hand shadow puppet shows?

Because they look SHADY!

What kind of game do you play when you can't play with a phone?

BORED games!

Why do ghosts eat organic food?

Because it's SUPER NATURAL!

Doctor! Doctor!

I stepped on a pile of Legos
in my bare feet!
Doctor: Try to BLOCK out the pain!

Doctor, Doctor!
Please help me.
I snore so loud I wake myself up!
Doctor: In that case, sleep in another
room.

How do you know when a bike
is thinking?

You can see its WHEELS TURNING.

What is a skunk's favorite video
game?

Fartnite.

Why can't skunks keep secrets?

Someone is always catching wind
of them!

Why do ducks have tail feathers?

To cover their butt-QUACKS.

How do ducks carry their drinks?

In a WADDLE bottle.

Finding my new kitten stuck up in a tree isn't the worst thing in the world.

But it's up there.

TWELVE.

multitasking
{muhl-ee-task-ing} verb.

Messing up several things
at the same time.

Ha
Ha
Ha

KNOCK, KNOCK!

Who's there?
Nana.
Nana who?
Nana your business!

How much memory does it take to store a joke?

One GIGGLEbyte.

This is Bob.
Bob has no arms.

"Knock, knock."
"Who is it?"
"It isn't Bob."

Ha
Ha
Ha
Ha

What superhero is a real pain in the neck?

BRAT-man!

Why didn't the teddy bear want dessert?

He was STUFFED.

What did the lawyer name his daughter?

Sue.

Little Bro: "I think I want to watch that new movie."

Big Bro: "What is it about?"

Little Bro: "I think it's about 2 hours."

What kind of water is healthy?

WELL water.

I would love to get paid for sleeping... it would be my dream job.

How do you make a rootbeer float?

Throw the can in the water!

Riddles!

1. What man cannot live in a house?

2. How can a moose cross the river without getting wet?

3. Where do four kings live if they are not in a castle?

4. How do you make two poop emojis out of one poop emoji?

1. A snowman. 2. The river is frozen.
3. In a deck of cards. 4. With a mirror.

18

Big Bro: Do you wanna fly?

Little Bro: Yes!

Big Bro: Okay, I'll catch one for you!

How do you get down from a unicorn?

You don't! You get DOWN from a DUCK.

Why did the bee have a big butt?

Because it was a BUM-ble bee!

I watched a sci-fi show that everyone
is talking about...

it was kind of weird but honestly, I've
seen STRANGER THINGS.

What do you give a vegan vampire?

A BLOOD ORANGE!

WAITER, WAITER!

Waiter, my soup is cold!
Waiter: It's Gazpacho, sir.
Diner: Gazpacho, my soup is cold!

Waiter, Waiter!
Waiter: You can have anything
you see on the menu.
Diner: Even the dirty fingerprints,
grease, and ketchup stains?

What is a werewolf's favorite
vegetable?

AROOOOOOgula!

What do you call a boy who
jokes all the time?

Josh.

What was the ballon animal's
last words to his dad?

Watch me POP!

Why did Snoopy quit working
for the comic strip?

He was tired of working for
Peanuts.

Fun Fact: Did you know you can't
breathe through your nose when
you are smiling?

LOL! Made you smile!

How do you make a taco stand?

Take away its chair!

What kind of cheese can never be yours?

NACHO cheese!

Our school childproofed the playground.

What are the kids going to do
at recess?

WARNING!
OFFICIAL
12
PRE-TEEN

hold your horses
[hohld yoo hawrses] phrase.

Imaginary horses that keep you from doing something that you really want to do.

Why can't computers drive cars?

Because they keep CRASHING.

Why can't Sponge Bob make the honor roll?

Because he is a C sponge!

Little Sis: "I want a King-sized bed."

Big Sis: "Why?"

Little Sis: "I want to dream BIG!"

How do you tickle a millionaire's baby?

Gucci, Gucci, Gucci Coo.

Well, that's not a good sign.

How do you cut the sea in half?

With a SEASAW!

What did the llama get when he graduated from school?

A dipLLAMA.

Ha Ha Ha

Why couldn't Mario find his cart?

It was TOAD!

Little Bro: "Why don't dinosaurs wear deodorant?"

Big Bro: "They don't want to be EX-STINK!"

What is a dinosaur's least favorite reindeer?

COMET!

Doctor! Doctor!

Everyone thinks that I am a liar!
Doctor: I find that hard to believe.

How do you stay alive in a heat wave?

THIRST things first.

My dog is a genius.

I asked him: "What is 10 X 0?"
"He said nothing!"

What do you buy for baby cats?

Dia-purrs!

What do you call a bankrupt cowboy?

DeRANGED.

What do you call a company started
by a few chimpanzees?

Monkey business.

I wouldn't do that if I were you
{i wood-nt doo that if i wur yuh] phrase.

A friend that reminds you of
your mom.

KNOCK, KNOCK!

Who's there?
Sea.
Sea who?
Sea you later, alligator!

Knock, knock.
Who's there?
Tank.
Tank who?
You're welcome!

Big Sis: "Why don't you wear snow boots?"

Little Sis: "Because they would MELT!"

What did the mom ghost say to
her kids?

It's tough being APPARENT!

What do you call a ghost's snot?

A BOOger.

Why do ghosts obsess over expensive
things?

Because they're super BOOugie.

Where is the best place in the house
to hide from a ghost?

The LIVING room!

Why don't people believe anything that a giraffe says?

Because they tell TALL tales.

Ha
Ha
Ha

The invisible man tried to lie to me.

But I saw right through him!

WAITER, WAITER!

There's a fly in my soup!
Waiter: Don't worry, the spider in your salad will take care of it.

Why did the s'more go to school?

To become a GRAHAM-mar expert!

My least favorite color is orange.

I hate it more than RED AND YELLOW COMBINED.

Why can you always tell what
Dr. Seuss will do next?

Because he is so EASY TO READ.

floordrobe
[flawr-drohb] noun.

The largest clothes container
you own.

What do you get if you cross a pig
and a centipede?

BACON and LEGS.

Why is it hard to find a camel in
the desert?

Because they are CAMELflaged!

What do you call a cow with a twist?

Beef Jerky!

Why are drones the best way to take pictures of mermaids?

Because they take ARIEL pictures!

What kind of car does a zombie drive?

A MONSTER truck.

Snow White made six dwarfs clean their bedrooms this weekend.

None of them were HAPPY.

Why are video game jokes
so much fun?

Because they work on so many LEVELS!

What rhymes with pew and stinks?

YOU.

So what if I can't spell Armageddon!

It's not like the END OF THE WORLD.

Riddles!

5. I have a head and a tail, but I am not alive. What am I?

6. What table can you eat?

7. If two's company, three's a crowd, what is four and five?

8. The more I appear, the less you can see. What am I?

9. What is easy to get into but hard to get out of?

5. A coin. 6. A vegetable. 7. Nine. 8. Darkness. 9. Trouble.

What do you call a satellite photo?

An Earth selfie!

What did the invisible man say to the class?

Look at the board and I will go through it again!

How do you put a little bounce in your step?

Drink SPRING water!

What is a zombie's favorite restaurant?

Five Guys.

What do you do if you are allergic
to seaweed?

Sea Kelp!

Little Sis: "We had a lot of deer
in our front yard today!"

Big Sis: "Yeah, I HERD!"

What is the laziest bug?

The BED BUG.

41

WAITER, WAITER!

I'm in a hurry!
Will the pizza be long?
Waiter: No sir, it will be round.

Waiter, Waiter! We are ready
to order our food!
Waiter: When will your guests arrive?
Diner: They're here. I'll be
dining with my taste BUDS.

Why did the girl get fired at the
hamburger restaurant?

She put her hair in a BUN.

I don't care if people don't like my art.

I just BRUSH them off.

How do you make a computer cry?

Delete its cookies.

My dad thinks that I am obsessed with deep space exploration.

What planet does he live on?

What do you call a nerdy pig?

A DORKY PORKY!

How can you make your money go
a long way?

Put it in a rocket ship.

Little Bro: "Where are you going?"

Big Bro: "Crazy, want to come?"

Why do aliens lose so many golf balls?

Too many BLACK HOLES!

Why was the zombie left-handed?

Because his right hand fell off!

What kind of cheese do skateboarders eat?

Shredded cheese.

Ha Ha Ha Ha

What does a zombie call a skateboader?

Meals on wheels.

What do pimples do when you sleep?

Nothing, they just ZIT there.

Big Sis: "Why do you have lipgloss on your forehead?"

Little Sis: "I'm trying to make-up my mind."

I took a video of my new boots.

It was very good FOOTAGE!

Why do trees hate taking tests?

The questions always STUMP them.

What do you do when two snails have a fight?

Let them SLUG it out!

Have you heard of the band 1023MB?

They haven't got a GIG yet!

tween
[tween] noun.

A person who is better prepared for a zombie apocalypse than for school tomorrow.

What is 278/3 + 599 – 23?

A headache!

We all hope that someday we can live in a world without plagiarism.

You may say I'm a dreamer.
But I'm not the only one.

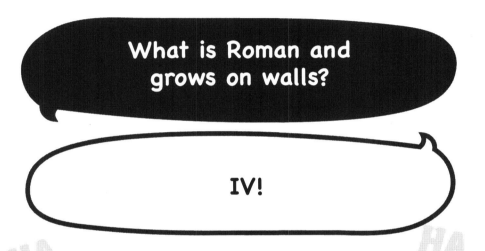

What is Roman and
grows on walls?

IV!

In a baseball game, would it take longer to run from 1st to 2nd base, or from 2nd to 3rd base?

It would take longer to run from 2nd to 3rd base because there's a SHORT-STOP in between!

What do you call a kid with a bug on his head?

Anton.

I like to bring my guitar with me when we go somewhere in the car.

It's good for traffic JAMS.

What do you call a sink with a shoe in it?

A CLOGGED sink.

A duck was standing on the curb
waiting for the walk sign to light up.
A chicken walked up to him and said,
"DON'T DO IT MAN,
you'll never hear
the end of it!"

Ha Ha
Ha Ha

How much does a Gen Z'er weigh?

An Instagram.

Why did the poop emoji
go to college?

To get a degree in
WASTE management!

Doctor! Doctor!

I think I am a small bucket!
Doctor: You are looking a little pale.

Student: " My dog ate my homework."

Computer Teacher: "Your dog ate
your coding assignment?"

Student: "Well, it did take him
a couple of BYTES!"

Why did the drummer go to bed early?

He was BEAT!

What's brown and sounds like a bell?

DUNG.

Why do people like slime jokes?

Because they're GOOO-great!

What insect is hard to understand?

A MUMBLE bee.

If a butcher's shirt size is XXL and he is 6 feet tall, what does he weigh?

MEAT. He's a butcher!

What do you call headphones that can't keep a charge?

DEADBEATS!

Big Bro: "I think you are overlooking something."

Little Bro: "What?"

Big Bro: "Your nose."

What is the most musical vegetable?

BEET-hoven!

What does a little zombie sleep
with?

A DEADY bear.

I didn't want to play with my
friend on Minecraft... so I
BLOCKED him.

What do baby zombies wear?

DIE-pers!

Super Soaker Water Gun fights may not improve your life.

But it's worth a SHOT!

Why are popsicles so snobby?

Because they have a stick up their butt.

KNOCK, KNOCK!

Who's there?
Tissue.
Tissue who?
All I want for Christmas tissue.

Knock, knock.
Who's there?
Why.
Why who?
Why-M-C-A!

Knock, knock.
Who's there?
Yah!
Yah who?
Settle down, cowboy!

? Riddles! ?

10. What is the smartest train in the world?

11. What happens to goblins when it rains?

12. What goes up and down, but never moves?

13. What has no beginning, end, or middle?

14. Voiceless it cries, toothless it bites. What am I?

14. The wind.
13. A doughnut.
12. A flight of stairs.
11. They get wet.
10. The train of thought.

Why don't you want lightning on your bowling team?

Because lightning never STRIKES twice!

Why do ghosts go to concerts?

They have the best SHEETS in the house!

Why did the witch stay home?

She had a WICKED cold.

farts
[fahrts] noun.

Ghosts of the things we eat.

How did the ballerina get the lead role in the play?

She was ON HER TOES!

What do you call 288 cafeteria lunches?

Two Gross!
(1 gross = 144 things)

Why don't astronauts bring skateboards into space?

Because they can't get AIR there!

How do trees find their ancestors?

They trace their ROOTS!

Why do giraffes sing in the rain?

Because they don't fit in the shower!

What do you call a thirsty giraffe?

High and dry!

Here's why
I HATE PASSWORDS

Windows: Please enter a new password.

User: tacos

Windows: Sorry, the password must be more than 8 characters.

User: cheese tacos

Windows: Sorry, the password must contain 1 numerical character.

User: 100 cheese tacos

Windows: Sorry, the password cannot have blank spaces.

User: 100dumbcheesetacos

Windows: Sorry, the password must contain at least 1 uppercase character.

User: 100DUMBcheesetacos

Windows: Sorry, the password cannot contain more than 1 uppercase character consecutively.

User: 100DumbCheeseTacosGiveMe AccessNowYouStupidIdiot!

Windows: Sorry, the password cannot contain punctuation.

User: IWillHuntYouDown100DumbCheese TacosGiveMeAccessNowYouStupidIdiot

Windows: Sorry, that password is already in use.

Why does anyone still want
a landline?

To call their cellphone when they
can't find it!

Teacher: "Why are you doing
your math homework on the floor?"

Student: "You told us we couldn't
use tables!"

Where do spiders look for health advice?

WebMD.

What state has the most baby
rodents?

New HAMPSTER!

WAITER, WAITER!

I need to order a drink with my meal.
Waiter: Of course, what would you like?
Diner: A blind rootbeer.
Waiter: Excuse me?
Diner: You know, a blind rootbeer, NO ICE.

Waiter, Waiter!
Diner: There is only one piece of meat on my plate.
Waiter: Just a moment, sir, and I'll cut it in two.

What is the heaviest soup?

Won TON soup.

What is better than summer vacation?

More summer vacation!

What do you call a vulture in the winter?

A BRRRRRd!

Big Bro: "What kind of food do they serve in your school cafeteria?"

Little Bro: "Mystery food!"

Stop pulling my leg!

Knock, knock.
Who's there?
Toad.
Toad who?
Toad you we were having
frog legs for lunch.

What social media does a musician use?

RAP-chat.

Why did the selfie go to prison?

It was FRAMED!

Don't trust atoms...they make up everything.

What do you call a hippo with a messy room?

A hippopota-MESS!

What do you call a ghost spell?

BOO-DOO!

Why isn't there any knock-knock jokes about freedom?

Because freedom RINGS!

Why did the teacher give the smart Alec student an A+?

He made a WISECRACK!

What did one car say to the car when it was raining?

I'm glad I have my HOOD on!

purgatory
[pur-guh-tawr-ee] noun.

Trying to untangle your charger cords.

Genie: What is your first wish?

Dude: I want to be rich.

Genie: What is your second wish, Rich?

Rich: Well, aren't you a Smarty Pants! I want 100 Billion dollars!

Smarty Pants: Now I have no powers! Way to go Rich, no powers, no third wish!

Genie: I can only grant you one wish.

Dude: I want to be happy.

Genie: Okay Happy. Say hi to Snow White for me, and have fun hanging out with the 6 dwarfs.

Why do marsupials have family game night every week?

Because they like to spend KOALA-ty time together!

How did the lacrosse player cross the road?

He used LACROSSE walk!

My older sister wants to be a pastry chef.

I hope she doesn't DESSERT her plans.

Riddles!

? ? ? ? ? ? ? ? ? ?

15. What kind of soda can't you drink?

16. What has three feet but no legs?

17. What is the loudest kind of pet?

18. What number and letter can spell "dog"?

19. What bird appears at every breakfast?

20. What kind of pie can fly?

15. Baking Soda. 16. A yard stick.
17. A trumpet. 18. K-9.
19. A swallow. 20. A magpie.

Mom: "How come you're not doing your chores?"

Son: "I didn't see you coming!"

What does an aardvark like on its pizza?

ANT-chovies.

If two wrongs don't make a right, what do two rights make?

An airplane!

What do you get if you cross a pickle with a dollar bill?

SOURDOUGH.

Tongue Twister

Dare you to repeat this 3x!

> Garden gargoyles grow gooey garlic.

What did the caveman order at the restaurant?

A CLUB sandwich.

Some kids aren't crazy about playing soccer.

They do it just for the KICKS.

JUST BE
HAPPY
I'M NOT A TWIN

What do you call a girl who doesn't apply enough suntan lotion?

Tanya.

What is Superman's favorite road?

Lois Lane.

How much time does it take to make a grandfather clock?

Don't know...but I bet it is time consuming!

Jokes about unemployed people
are not funny.

They just DON'T WORK.

Little Bro: "What is the best snack to
eat during a scary movie?"

Big Bro: "Ice Scream!"

Squirrels have a habit of storing
food in the winter.

Isn't that NUTS!

"Hey Ernie, would you like some ice cream?"

"Sure, Bert."

What is a vampire's favorite ice cream flavor?

VEINilla.

Why do ice cream cones usually carry an umbrella?

There may be a chance of SPRINKLES.

Why is ice cream so bad at tennis?

They have SOFT SERVE.

Why is it hard to make friends in computer class?

Because everyone is too CLICKY!

Big Sis: "Hey, Mom wants us to help her fix dinner."

Little Sis: "I didn't know it was broken!"

What did the fireman name his two sons?

José and Hose B!

WAITER, WAITER!

Waiter: Yes sir, how may I help you?
Diner: This salad is frozen!
Waiter: That's because it
is made with ICEBURG lettuce, sir.

I hate it when people gossip
in the kitchen.

All they do is stand there and STIR
THE POT!

Waiter, Waiter! There is a BEE
in my soup!
Waiter: Of course, sir. It's alphabet
soup.

Why did the tree go home early?

It had to LEAF.

What kind of flower do you get
when you cross a pointer
and a setter?

A poinsettia!

What big cat hangs around
in the backyard?

The clothes-LION.

If a gardener has a green thumb,
who has a purple and blue thumb?

A near-sighted carpenter.

Who do mermaids date?

They go out with the TIDE.

What kind of money do elves make?

Jingle BILLS.

What did the witch think about her boyfriend?

She was SPELLbound.

Why don't witches like to ride their brooms when they're angry?

They are afraid of flying off the handle!

Doctor! Doctor!

I feel like a lightning bolt!
Doctor: That's shocking!

Doctor, Doctor!
Why is that man hanging from the ceiling by one arm?
Doctor: Don't worry about him, he thinks he's a lightbulb.
Patient: Well, why don't you tell him that he's not a lightbulb?
Doctor: What? And work in the dark?

How did the doctors cure the Invisible Man?

They took him to the ICU.

Why can't a clock keep secrets?

Because TIME WILL TELL.

What kind of teeth can you buy for a dollar?

BUCK teeth.

Why is it hard to drive a field hockey ball?

Because it doesn't have a steering wheel!

What do you call a girl who is full of herself?

Mimi.

KNOCK, KNOCK!

Who's there?
Pecan.
Pecan who?
Pecan someone your own size!

Knock, knock.
Who's there?
Pencil.
Pencil who?
Pencil fall down if you don't wear
a belt!

Knock, knock.
Who's there?
Artichokes.
Artichokes who?
Artichokes when he eats
too fast!

Where do mermaids go to see a movie?

The DIVE-in.

What does Spiderman do on his day off?

He surfs the WEB.

Why aren't lifeguards good at saving hippies?

Because they're too FAR OUT!

What letter is the coolest?

Iced T!

What word has 3 syllables
and contains 26 letters?

Alphabet!

What city cheats
on exams?

Peking!

Tongue
Twister

Dare you to repeat this 3x!

Cheeky chickens chew
cheesy cherries.

What do you call a boy who likes
automobiles?

Carson.

When is it a funny time to take milk and sugar with your tea?

Tee-Hee time.

Voldemort: "So that's all you have to do is...lie?"

Pinocchio: "Yep."

What did the pants say to the kid?

You're putting me on!

What did the glass blower name his daughter?

Crystal!

What did the hostile pizza say?

"You want a piece of me?"

What does a detective name his dog?

Snoopy!

Lunges are a good exercise to try.

Yeah, I know, it's a big step forward.

How do you make a fruit roll?

You push it!

What do you call a skeptical fashion designer?

CLOTHES-minded!

What do you call a man with a shovel?

Doug.

What do you call a man without a shovel?

Douglas.

What is the best way
to burn calories?

Leave the chocolate
chip cookies in the oven
too long!

Why did the music note
drop out of college?

Because it couldn't
pick a MAJOR!

What do you call an
obnoxious reindeer?

RUDE-olph!

What is the scariest
word in nuclear physics?

OOPS!

Riddles!

21. What goes into a birdbath but never gets wet?

22. What can you break, even if you never pick it up or touch it?

23. What kind of room has no doors or windows?

24. When the water comes down, I go up. What am I?

25. Is it possible for a tween to go 7 days without sleeping?

21. The bird's shadow. 22. A promise.
23. A mushroom. 24. An umbrella.
25. Yes, the tween will sleep at night.

WAITER, WAITER!

Why does my chocolate cake look
like a car ran over it?
Waiter: Sir, you did ask me to
step on it!

What's a goblin's favorite dinner?

GHOULash!

Waiter, Waiter!
What is this fly doing in my soup?
Waiter: Sir, I believe it's doing
the backstroke!

What do you call two earthworms in love?

SOIL mates!

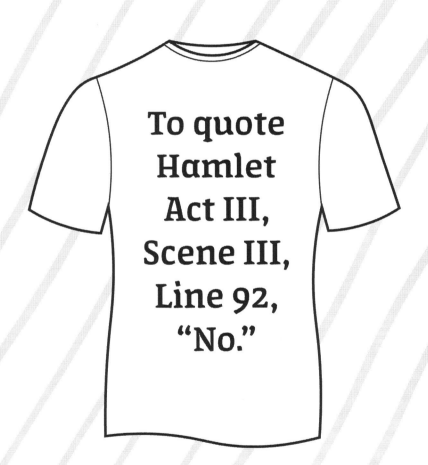

To quote
Hamlet
Act III,
Scene III,
Line 92,
"No."

How do you confront a hurricane?

Look it in the EYE!

Why don't snails fart?

Their houses don't have windows.

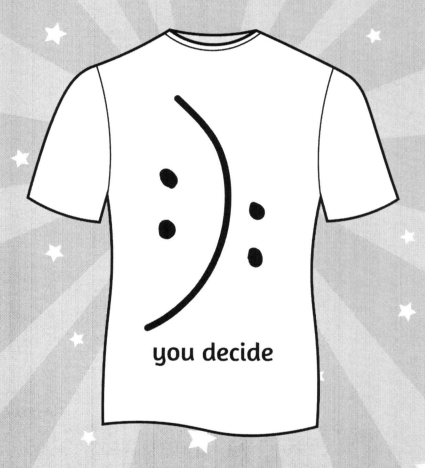

you decide

What is Bigfoot's favorite book?

HAIRY Potter!

KNOCK, KNOCK!

Who's there?
Scott.
Scott who?
Scott nothing to say to you!

Knock, knock.
Who's there?
Little girl.
Little girl who?
Little girl who cannot reach
the doorbell!

Knock, knock.
Who's there?
Salami.
Salami who?
Salami get this straight..you don't like
knock-knock jokes?

Doctor! Doctor!

I think I'm a dog!
Doctor: Please hop up on the
examination table.
Patient: I can't, I'm not allowed
on the furniture.

A skeleton walked into the
doctor's office.
Doctor: Aren't you a little late?

PULL YOURSELF
TOGETHER MAN!

What kind of hawk has no beak?

A tomahawk.

Big Bro: "Why are you eating your homework?"

Little Bro: "The teacher said it was a piece of cake!

What do you call a boy with no shins?

Tony.

What superhero is the best house-flipper?

The Incredible Hulk!

Where does Cyclops go after
5th grade?

Junior EYE school!

Who takes care of a graveyard?

A SCARE-taker!

What do you call a group of ghosts
watching a baseball game?

SPOOK-tators!

What happens when a monster goes
to the bathroom?

Cree-Pee!

Why did the black cat join the drama club?

Because she was a PURR-former!

How often do werewolves get together?

Once in a blue moon.

Who works the graveyard shift in the cemetry?

The SKELETON crew!

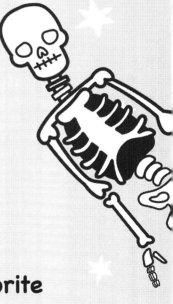

What is the ghost's favorite week of school?

SPIRIT week!

What is the key to writing dwarf jokes?

Keep them SHORT.

What do golfers like to drink
on a hot day?

Iced TEE.

Why didn't the quarter jump off
of the hill after the nickel?

Because it had more CENTS!

Mother Earth is to blame for
all of the earthquakes...
it is her FAULT.

Why was the monster under the bed in trouble?

He was under A REST.

What do you call a bear that works at a coffee shop?

A BEAR-ista.

What is the coldest meal during the day?

Brrrr-eakfast!

Why did King Arthur
have a round table?

So nobody could
CORNER him!

Who built King Authur's
round table?

Sir CUMFERENCE!

What did King George
think of the American colonists?

He thought they were REVOLTING!

What kind of tea did the American
colonists want at the Boston Tea Party?

Liberty!

I overheard someone on the bus telling Pokemon jokes.

But I couldn't CATCH them all!

Little Sis: "What did the vegetable wear to the beach?

Big Sis: "A Zu-kini!

What do you call it when you finish your tea?

Tea end!

Books From Tesse Adams

Hilarious Joke Books!

Made in the USA
Middletown, DE
04 September 2023

37948974R00062